69 Exquisite Ways to Eat Cock

Healthy Chicken Recipes to Leave Your Guests Wanting More

Kate Marlow

Copyright © 2021 Kate Marlow

All rights reserved. No part of this publication may be reproduced, distributed, or transmitted in any form or by any means, including photocopying, recording, or other electronic or mechanical methods, without the prior written permission of the publisher, except in the case of brief quotations embodied in critical reviews and certain other noncommercial uses permitted by copyright law.

Limit of Liability/Disclaimer of Warranty: While the publisher and author have used their best efforts in preparing this book, they make no representations or warranties with respect to the accuracy or completeness of the contents of this book and specifically disclaim any implied warranties of merchantability or fitness for a particular purpose. No warranty may be created or extended by sales representatives or written sales materials. The advice and strategies contained herein may not be suitable for your situation. You should consult with a professional where appropriate. Neither the publisher nor author shall be liable for any loss of profit or any other commercial damages, including but not limited to special, incidental, consequential, or other damages.

ISBN: 9798474479972

DEDICATION

To Alan

Love you now and always!

TABLE OF CONTENTS

INTRODUCTION 1

    Helpful Tips That Might Come In Handy 3

    To Peel or Not To Peel? 3

    How to Identify a Fresh Apple 4

    Peeling and Coring an Apple 5

    Slicing an Uncored Apple 6

    Storing Apples 6

    Keeping the Apple from Turing Brown 7

BREAKFAST 8

    Basic Crepes 9

   10

    Apple Cranberry Oatmeal 10

    Apple Puff omelet 12

    Apple Frittata 14

    Breakfast Sausage Crepes 15

   16

    Apple Ring Fritters 16

   18

    Apple Doughnuts 18

    SOUPS AND STARTERS 20

   20

    Sweet Potato Apple and Ginger Soup 20

    Chestnut Soup with Spiced Apple-Cranberry Compote 22

    Chicken Liver Pate with Apple 23

Bacon Wrapped Dates with Curried Apple Hash 25

BREAD 27

Coffee Can Bread 28

Whole-Wheat Nut Quick Bread 30

Apple Tea Bread 32

Apple Banana Bread 34

Apple Coffee Cake 36

DESSERTS 38

Johnny Appleseed Squares 39

Baked Apple Slices 40

Caramel Apple Puff Dumplings 42

Apricot Apple Dumplings 44

Applesauce Brownies 45

Apple Bread Pudding 47

Apple and Date Squares 49

Sherried Apple Crêpes 51

Apple Molasses Cookies 53

Caramel Toffee Apples 54

PIES, CAKES AND MUFFINS 56

.... 56

    Oatmeal Apple Cupcakes 57

    Apple Lemon Cake 59

.... 61

    Chocolate Applesauce Cake 61

    Apple Nut Cake 63

    Quick Apple Cake 65

.... 67

    Bran Applesauce Muffins 67

SALADS AND SIDES 69

    Apple and Parmesan Curl Salad 70

    Spinach Apple Salad 71

.... 72

    Waldorf Salad 72

    Stuffed Apple Salad 74

.... 76

    Apple Tortellini Salad 76

    Potato Apple Salad 78

    Curried Chicken Salad 79

CHICKEN, FISH & MORE 81

    Tuna Apple Tortilla Wraps 82

    Grilled Tuna with Apple Chutney 83

    Sea Scallops with Coriander & Cider Sauce 85

    Roast Chicken with Apples Turnips and Garlic 87

    Pork Chops with Apple Cream Sauce 88

Pork Tenderloin with Apple Shallot Sauce 90

Pork tenderloin stuffed with apples 92

Curried Ham and Apples 94

DRINKS AND COCKTAILS 95

Party Apple Punch 96

Wassail 97

Apple Eggnog 98

Fruit Crush 99

Jack Rose Cocktail 101

Coming in From the Cold Cocktail 102

Apple Cucumber Lime and Mint Salsa 103

Mulled Apple Cider 104

INTRODUCTION

Chicken has been a staple all over the world from the time of the Romans to the time of the 'rona. From chicken curry to chicken nuggets and fried chicken then roast chicken, we have continually enjoyed tearing apart some chicken and eating them all up, down to cracking the bones. As teenagers, we had picnics with chicken, in a family gathering, chicken roast and when huddled up ready to enjoy a good Netflix movie, we get chicken nuggets.

Chicken is the thing you can sneak into your kitchen at night to steal or it could be the reliable dish you could order at your local restaurant.

Over the years, I have been interested in chicken food poultry and even experimented in raising a pair of homegrown hens (an interesting experience). The result made me understand that the secret to a good chicken was in the ability to experiment and substitute other recipes. I documented my experience in this book so you could prepare from scratch a restaurant standard golden, crisp-skinned piece of chicken.

Nothing is too difficult to cook. Each recipe contains short, straight to the point pieces of writing that show you succinctly, how chicken is easy and there is really no reason to follow elaborate styles and complicate your kitchen experience. This book could have been five times the size, but less is more and i thought it was better to have a useful book with a catchy title that reminds you every time that there are interesting ways to eat chicken instead of the same old, same old.

All recipes here are regulars in the kitchen and i hope they become regulars in yours too, so much that you enjoy it enough to experiment with it and create your own delicious variation.

Enjoy!

Every chicken on earth is a descendant of the red jungle fowl, a jungle bird that lives in south Asia. It was a small, very hard to find bird that once captured was cooked immediately because the birds were very shy of humans and prolonged contacts with humans almost always resulted in a heart attack.

The Red Jungle Fowl

Chickens have also impacted early civilizations. From around 500 BC, Themistocles, an Athenian general on his way to war against the Persian forces, stopped to watch two cocks fighting, amazed by the pointless but instinctive aggression showed, they were so inspired that they decided to emulate the aggression in their battle. History recorded the Greeks finally went on to win the war and repel the invaders.

In Ancient Babylon, around 800 B.C, the ancient Babylonians considered the chicken sacred. It was a symbol of rebirth, both spiritual and physical simply because it crowed around dawn just before the light appeared.

In Rome, the behavior of chickens were observed thoroughly before going to battle; if the chicken had a good appetite, victory was sure. But if they didn't then it meant defeat was certain. According to dug up writings of Cicero, in 249 B.C, a consul preparing to go to war consulted the birds but this time they refused to eat, angry, he threw them overboard and he was subsequently defeated. It is unknown if this was a cautionary tale but the fact still remains that the birds were of great importance then.

In Christianity, in Matthew 23:37, Jesus likened his affection for the people of Jerusalem as a hen caring for her brood. Even the chicken played an important role in fulfilling the prophecy that peter would deny Jesus 'before the cock crows three times'

Pope Nicholas I also influenced the popularity of the rooster by decreeing a figure of a rooster be placed atop every church as a reminder of the incident, this singular decree led to the popularity of rooster-shaped weather vanes and created a whole industry, albeit briefly.

Culturally, African-Americans have a deep historical knowledge of the chicken. Before they were brought from West Africa, they had the chicken as a common farm animals and their knowledge helped them during the colonial times when there were few other things to eat.

Gradually, they began to raise chickens and sell them to other slave owners who would give their slaves to prepare for them. As the whites began to get a taste for chicken, they began to like fried chicken and many more delicacies and over time, chicken became one of the most important cuisines of that region.

NUTRITION

From soup preparations to fried, dried or roasted forms, Chicken is a very excellent source of low-calorie/low fat but incredibly high quality protein content that provides all the necessary nutrition all through our lives and in all part of our body. Here's a quick run through of both the health and nutritional benefits of chicken.

The Brain

Chicken meat contains vitamin B12 and choline, which in children actively aids in brain development and for adults, promotes cognitive performance.

Bones

Scientists had previously believed that a chicken rich diet could reduce bone density particularly in children and older people. However this has recently been debunked in a 20q6 nutrition study that shows chicken meat works hand in hand with calcium to protect the bones and keep them strong and healthy. Also it has a high amount of selenium which has been known to help reduce the risk of arthritis

Mood

Chicken contains tryptophan, an amino acid responsible for regulating the serotonin levels in the brain and producing a calming effect on your body, consuming chicken regularly raises your serotonin levels and makes you 'feel-good'. Chicken definitely makes for an excellent option after a stressful day.

Builds Muscle

Chicken is a source of high quality dietary protein. It is lean meat, which means that it contains more protein and really low amounts of fat. 30 grams of chicken per meal could greatly improve muscle growth, great for those who would want to bulk up

Increase Testosterone Levels

Men should consume foods rich in zinc as it helps boost testosterone levels as well as boost sperm production.

Weight Loss

Chicken meat is an excellent source of protein that the body converts easily

BEST COOKING PRACTICES

Buying the Best Chicken

An important but overlooked part of preparing chicken is buying the best chicken, buying the best chicken be sure to check the 'sell' date so you do not buy a chicken that is almost at the end of its shelf life.

Another helpful tip is to inspect the package of the chicken, if it feels sticky or contains some liquid or even the faintest whiff of odor, it should be discarded.

Avoid frozen chicken with ice around it, why? Chicken tastes best when it has not been frozen for long. Most poultry are frozen before they get to the store, so it gets frozen twice and lasts for longer periods to prolong shelf life leading to damaged texture and flavor.

Storing and Freezing

Chicken should ideally be eaten within a day or two of its purchase from the store, in case your chicken needs to be stored, it should be placed in its original package and placed at the back of the fridge, where it is coldest and is not readily accessible to hands accessing the refrigerator. A freezer temperature of 0 F can prolong the shelf life of a chicken for up to six months, but for the best taste, it is ideal to cook within a month.

Under thawing is a common mistake people tend to make when defrosting whole birds, the chicken gets defrosted on the outside while the center remains frozen, this tends to affect your cooking.

In preparing to cook frozen chicken, it should be thawed first in cold water for two to eight hours depending on weight and size with the water changed regularly. To check if the chicken is defrosted wiggle the wings and legs to see if they move freely and the flesh squishy.

I hope this cookbook becomes a staple in your kitchen and becomes a source of many happy meals and interesting conversations like it did to me, with this cookbook, a good meal is never far away.

Enjoy

Chicken Jerk

Cook Time: 8 hours 20minutes

Prep Time: 10 minutes

Total Time: 8 hours 30minutes

Servings: 4 people

Ingredients:

½ white onion (minced)

1 teaspoon allspice powder

¼ cup orange juice or any other citrus

¼ teaspoon cinnamon

1 tablespoon minced ginger

½ teaspoon clove powder

1 tablespoon jalapeno (minced)

2 to 3 pounds whole cock, broken down to pieces

1 tablespoon soy sauce

2 tablespoon minced garlic.

Instructions:

1. In a bowl, combine the cloves, onions, cinnamon, orange juice, allspice, ginger, garlic, pepper and soy sauce. Mix evenly for your marinade.

2. Place cock in marinade. Seal tightly and place in the fridge for 7 to 8 hours.
3. Set your grill at medium heat. Place your cock on the grill and cook for 8 minutes on each side.
4. For your glaze, cook what's left of your marinade on medium heat for 5 minutes. Enjoy.

Kingston Chicken Curry

Cook Time: 50 minutes

Prep Time: 10 minutes

Total Time: 1 hour

Servings: 6 people

Ingredients

½ cup curry, divided

3 cups water

3 tablespoon of garlic powder

1 Irish potato diced

2 tablespoon salt

1 tablespoon onion powder

1 tablespoon minced ginger

2 big carrots, chopped

2 green onions, chopped

2 teaspoons chopped scotch bonnet

1 sprig fresh rosemary

1 tablespoon black pepper

2 ¼ pounds of whole cock, broken down to pieces

3 tablespoon of olive oil

Instructions:

1. Place your cock in a bowl with pepper, salt, 3 tablespoons of curry, garlic, rosemary, onion powder and combine.
2. In a frying pan, combine your oil with 2 tablespoon of curry. Heat up for 3 minutes on low heat.
3. Place your cock in the pan add in the carrots, green onions, water, potato, scotch bonnet, ginger and stir. Increase heat to medium. Temperature should be no more than 165°
4. Cover the pan and let the cock simmer for 45 minutes.
5. Remove cock for plating. Serve with gravy.

Jamaican Wings

Cook Time: 2 hours

Prep Time: 25 minutes

Total Time: 12 hours 25 minutes

Servings: 8 people

Ingredients:

3 tablespoons Jamaican jerk seasoning

1 green onion, chopped roughly

12 pickled jalapenos, sliced

3 diced garlic

2 tablespoons minced ginger

4 pounds cock wings

3 tablespoons of vegetable oil

Instructions:

1. In a blender, combine the following ingredients till smooth; sliced jalapenos, garlic, ginger, onion, Jamaican jerk seasoning and vegetable oil.
2. Turn paste into a Ziploc bag and add cock wings. Shake to ensure paste is evenly distributed. Put in the fridge overnight.
3. Preheat oven at 185° for 10 minutes.
4. Place the wings in the oven and bake at 300° for 1 hour 45 minutes. Enjoy

Tasty Caribbean Styled Fettuccine

Prep Time: 10 minutes

Cook Time: 35 minutes

Total Time: 45 minutes

Servings: 2 people

Ingredients

1 tablespoon olive oil

1 teaspoon cinnamon

1 teaspoon chili flakes

2 cock breast, deboned

½ teaspoon red pepper flakes

1 (8 ounce) canned pineapple

¼ cup of coconut, shredded

2 tablespoons brown sugar

4 ounces of fettuccine

Salt to taste

Instructions:

1. Boil pasta in salted water for 9 minutes. Strain and set aside.
2. In a heated pan, add oil and cock. Stir fry for 12 minutes.
3. Add in pepper, cinnamon, canned pineapple, brown sugar, chili flakes, salt, red pepper flakes and coconut. Allow to simmer for 15 minutes.
4. Combine pasta with the sauce and stir for even distribution. Reduce heat to low and cook for 2 minutes. Enjoy

Sweet And Spicy Chicken

Prep Time: 5 minutes

Cook Time: 1 hour

Total Time: 1 hour 5 minutes

Serving: 4 people

Ingredients

½ cup of Sriracha sauce

2 tablespoons baking powder

1 tablespoon kosher salt

1 tablespoon rice vinegar

1 teaspoon ground black pepper

1/3 teaspoon sesame oil

2 pinches of sesame seeds

1/3 cup honey

1 teaspoon smoked paprika

2 ½ pounds cock wings

Instructions:

1. Preheat an oven at 425°. Cover your dish with foil.
2. Mix the paprika, salt, baking powder and ground black pepper in a bowl.
3. Add wings into the bowl and knead with your hands. Ensure that each wing is covered with seasoning.

4. Transfer wings to the dish and place in the oven for 22 minutes before flipping to the other side for another 22 minutes. Flip them one last time and cook for 10 minutes.
5. In a 2nd bowl, mix the sesame oil, honey, Sriracha sauce and vinegar. Add wings and toss.
6. Plate your wings and pour what's left of the sauce on them

Buffalo Soup

Prep Time: 10 minutes

Cook Time: 35 minutes

Total Time: 45 minutes

Servings: 4

Ingredients

½ cup buffalo sauce

¾ cup of milk

2 chopped green onions

4 ounces processed cheese

½ tablespoon cayenne pepper

¼ cup of butter

3 chopped celery

½ tablespoon celery salt

¼ cup of flour

½ teaspoon garlic salt

¾ cup cock broth

3 cups cooked cock, diced into equal pieces

Instructions:

1. In a skillet, melt your butter. Add in celery and onions. Stir till tender then stir in the flour.
2. Whisk the milk and cock broth together and slowly combine it with your ingredients in the pan.
3. After the broth and milk are well incorporated, add the following ingredients to the pan; cock, green onion, cheese, cayenne pepper, celery salt, garlic salt and buffalo sauce.
4. Continue cooking on steady heat till you find that the cheese and all other ingredients are combined beautifully. Enjoy.

September's Fajitas

Prep Time: 10 minutes

Cook Time: 6 hours

Total Time: 6 hours 10 minutes

Servings: 6 people

Ingredients

½ cup olive oil

½ cup distilled white vinegar

½ cup lime juice

1 red onion, sliced

1 bell pepper, sliced

14 ounces dry Italian salad dressing mix

3 whole boneless skinless cock, broken down to pieces

Instructions:

1. Mix the olive oil, dry Italian dressing mix, vinegar and lime juice in a bowl. Add in the cock quickly followed by bell pepper and onion. Make sure to coat each piece of cock properly.
2. Seal the bowl with a lid and leave in the fridge for 6 hours.
3. Remove the cock, bell pepper and onions from the marinade and fry in a pan with heated oil till done. Remove and plate. Enjoy.

Easy Asian Styled Chicken

Prep Time: 10 minutes

Cook Time: 10 minutes

Total Time: 20 minutes

Servings: 4 people

Ingredients

1 pound boneless cock breast

½ teaspoon garlic powder

1 egg

¼ teaspoon ground black pepper

½ teaspoon onion powder

1 cup panko crumbs

¼ cup corn oil

½ sea salt

Instructions:

1. Make a mix with onion powder, garlic powder, salt, panko and black pepper.
2. Flatten your cock and dip in whisked eggs before coating them with seasoning mix.
3. Fry cock for 4 minutes on each side in hot oil.
4. Drain off excess oil with paper towel. Enjoy.

Rustic Style Chicken

Prep Time: 15 minutes

Cook Time: 50 minutes

Total Time: 1 hour 5 minutes

Servings: 4 people

Ingredients

¼ cup butter

½ teaspoon paprika

1 teaspoon lemon thyme

4 potatoes cut in inch thick cubes

2 cock breasts

½ teaspoon garlic powder

4 carrots cut in ½ inch thick slices

½ teaspoon white pepper

3 celery stalks cut in ½ inch slices

1 tablespoon rosemary

½ teaspoon seasoned salt

Salt and black pepper to taste

Instructions:

1. In a bowl add your roughly chopped thyme and rosemary along with the salt, black pepper, white pepper, paprika, garlic powder and seasoned salt.

2. Melt the butter in a pan and baste for 6 minutes. Turn the cock over and add your carrots, potatoes and celery.
3. Add in your thyme mix and cover. Leave on medium heat for 47 minutes. Ensure your cock cools down to an internal temperature of 165°. Enjoy.

Savoury Garlic Chicken Breast

Prep Time: 5 minutes

Cook Time: 35 minutes

Total Time: 40 minutes

Servings: 4 people

Ingredients

1 tablespoon lemon extract

1 tablespoon minced garlic

¾ cup cock broth

4 cock breast halves, deboned

Cooking spray

Salt and black pepper to taste

Instructions:

1. Coat your pot with cooking spray and place on medium heat. Add your minced garlic and stir fry.
2. Season your cock with salt and pepper and place them in the pot. Add your lemon extract and broth. Cook for 14 minutes.
3. Bring to low heat when the pot comes to a boil, cover with a lid and leave to simmer for 17 minutes. Your cock is ready.
4. For a glaze, boil your broth for 5 more minutes till reduced. Enjoy.

Chicken Breast Dump Dinner

Prep Time: 10 minutes

Cook Time: 8 hours 10 minutes

Total Time: 8hours 20 minutes

Servings: 4 people

Ingredients

½ white onion, chopped

1 garlic clove, minced

14.5 ounce canned diced tomatoes

1 teaspoon Italian seasoning

1 pound cock breast halves, deboned

Instructions:

1. Place your pot on low heat. Put in the cock, garlic, Italian seasoning, diced tomatoes and onions
2. Leave this on the slow cooker for 8 hours. Then leave uncovered for 10 minutes before adding salt and pepper to your desired taste. Enjoy.

Carrots, Peppers and Parsley Chicken Breast

Prep Time: 10 minutes

Cook Time: 40 minutes

Total Time: 50 minutes

Servings: 4 people

Ingredients

1 teaspoon salt

½ cup olive oil

7 green onions, chopped

1 teaspoon Italian seasoning

8 carrots cut into ½ thick slices

1 teaspoon chili flakes

1 teaspoon lemon pepper

⅓ teaspoon ground black pepper

4 boneless cock breasts

4 green bell peppers, chopped

¼ cup chopped fresh parsley

Instructions:

1. Preheat oven at 375° before anything else.
2. In a cast iron skillet, layer your cock followed by the parsley, carrots, onions, celery, bell peppers, black and lemon pepper, chili flakes and Italian seasoning.
3. Place in the oven to cook for 40 minutes. Enjoy.

Bite Sized Baked Chicken

Prep Time: 10 minutes

Cook Time: 30 minutes

Total Time: 40 minutes

Servings: 4 people

Ingredients

1½ cup seasoned bread crumbs

4 tablespoons melted butter

1 pound cock breast, cut into bite sized pieces

Instructions:

1. Preheat oven at 325°.
2. Coat the cock with melted butter then dip into your seasoned bread crumbs.
3. Grill cock in the oven for 12 minutes. Flip over and grill for 10 more minutes. Enjoy.

Pineapple, Lime and Garlic Chicken

Prep Time: 10 minutes

Cook Time: 8 hours 40 minutes

Total Time: 8 hours 50 minutes

Servings: 2 people

Ingredients

½ cup diced pineapples

1 tablespoon garlic, minced

¼ cup olive oil

⅓ cup lime juice

2 boneless cock breast halves

Salt and black pepper to taste

Instructions:

1. In a bowl, combine the black pepper, salt, garlic, lime juice, olive oil with the cock. Place in the fridge overnight.
2. Preheat oven to 375° before anything else.
3. Transfer cock to a pan and season with additional salt and black pepper. Bake for 35 minutes. Add your diced pineapples and bake for 5 more minutes.
4. Plate your cock and enjoy.

BbQ Style Chicken

Prep Time: 50 minutes

Cook Time: 20 minutes

Total Time: 1 hour 10 minutes

Servings: 2 people

Ingredients

1 bottle barbecue sauce

1 cup Italian salad dressing

2 cock breasts

Salt and pepper to taste

Instructions:

1. In a bowl, place your cock, salad dressing, pepper and salt. Place in the fridge for 45 minutes.
2. Get your grill heated and coat with cooking spray.
3. Place cock on the grill and cook for 8 minutes on each side. Coat the cock liberally with barbecue sauce.
4. Plate and enjoy.

Chipotle Themed Cock

Prep Time: 10 minutes

Cook Time: 6 hours 20 minutes

Total Time: 6 hours 30 minutes

Servings: 4 people

Ingredients

2 tablespoons smoked paprika

2 teaspoon minced garlic

1 tablespoon olive oil

1 teaspoon cumin

1 teaspoon caraway seeds

1 teaspoon harissa

1 chipotle pepper adobo sauce

4 cock breasts, deboned

Salt and pepper to taste

Instructions:

1. In a mortar, mash the cumin, caraway seeds, paprika, garlic and chipotle pepper adobo sauce. Coat your cock with this paste.
2. Place cock in an air tight bowl and place in the fridge for 6 hours.

3. Remove cock and season with salt pepper and olive oil before grilling for 7 minutes on each side. Enjoy. Eat alone or with rice.

Orange Cinnamon Cock

Prep Time: 5 hours

Cook Time: 2 hour 5 minutes

Total Time: 7 hours 5 minutes

Servings: 4 people

Ingredients

½ cup harissa

½ cup orange juice

1 teaspoon cinnamon

2 teaspoons sugar

¼ cup apple cider vinegar

1 tablespoon orange zest

3 pound cock

3 tablespoons olive oil

Instructions:

1. Combine the following ingredients in a bowl till smooth; orange juice, harissa, cider vinegar, olive oil, sugar, orange zest and cinnamon. Coat your cock with this paste and place in a casserole dish.
2. Top cock with remaining mix, seal tight and place in the fridge for 5 hours

3. Preheat oven at 350°. Put your casserole in the oven for 2 hours. Baste every 20 minutes. Plate and enjoy.

Garlicky Bok Choy

Prep Time: 5 minutes

Cook Time: 15minutes

Total Time: 20minutes

Servings: 3 people

Ingredients

6 heads baby bok choy

¼ cup garlic, minced

2 tablespoons butter

2(14 ounce) can cock broth

⅓ tablespoon ground black pepper

Salt to taste

Instructions:

1. Place a pot on the stove on medium heat, melt butter and turn in the garlic. Stir fry for 5 minutes.
2. Add the cock broth and as your pot comes to boil, add the baby bok choy, salt and black pepper.
3. Bring pot to low heat and let it simmer for 5 minutes before plating.

Hangzhou Soup

Prep Time: 15 minutes

Cook Time: 40 minutes

Total Time: 55 minutes

Servings: 8 people

Ingredients

6 large bok choy leaves chopped finely

1 red onion, sliced

1 tablespoon olive oil

2 tablespoons minced garlic

2 celery stalks, cut into ½ inch thick slices

2 teaspoons cock soup base

5 small potatoes, cut into 1 inch thick cubes

6 cups water

4 carrots, sliced

2 cock breast halves, deboned

Instructions:

1. Saute onion and on low heat for 10 minutes before adding water, cock broth base, potatoes, carrots, bok choy and celery. Bring to a boil
2. Reduce heat and leave to boil for 10 minutes. Add the cock.
3. Leave to simmer for about 15 minutes. Enjoy.

Cajun Linguine

Prep Time: 20 minutes

Cook Time: 35 minutes

Total Time: 55 minutes

Servings: 2 people

Ingredients

4 ounces of linguine pasta

2 boneless cock breast halves

¼ teaspoon basil

¼ lemon pepper

2 teaspoons Cajun seasoning

¼ cup of parmesan cheese

¼ teaspoon salt

2 tablespoons butter

⅛ teaspoon garlic powder

⅓ ground black pepper

1 red bell pepper, chopped

4 mushrooms, chopped

1 cup heavy cream

Instructions:

1. Boil the pasta for 10 minutes then strain.
2. In a separate bowl, combine cock and Cajun seasoning. Stir fry cock in melted butter for 10 minutes
3. Toss in the bell peppers, mushrooms, green onions and continue to cook for 5 minutes before reducing the heat
4. Add your garlic powder, salt, basil, black pepper, cream and lemon pepper. Make sure all spices are incorporated properly.
5. Add your pasta to the mix and stir continuously for 3 minutes. Too with your Parmesan cheese. Enjoy.

Creamy Coconut Chicken

Prep Time: 15 minutes

Cook Time: 45 minutes

Total Time: 1 hour

Servings: 4 people

Ingredients

1 bunch fresh parsley, chopped roughly

14 ounce canned coconut milk

3 tomatoes, chopped

2 garlic cloves, minced

1 teaspoon turmeric powder

1 teaspoon cumin

1 teaspoon ground coriander

1 teaspoon cayenne pepper

1 tablespoon minced ginger

2 jalapeno peppers, sliced

1 white onion, chopped

4 cock breast halves, deboned

2 tablespoons olive oil

Salt and pepper to taste.

Instructions:

1. Place cock in a bowl alongside the cumin, cayenne pepper, salt, turmeric, pepper and coriander. Coat cock evenly.
2. In pan sear the cock with 1 tablespoon olive oil for 10 minutes on each side. Remove and set aside.
3. In the same pan, add remaining oil, onions, ginger, garlic and jalapeno peppers. Cook for 8 minutes.
4. Add in the tomatoes and cook for another 5 minutes. Stir in your coconut milk.
5. Pour sauce on the cock. Garnish with chopped parsley. Enjoy.

Onions, Carrots and Rosemary Chicken

Prep Time: 10 minutes

Cook Time: 1 hour 20 minutes

Total Time: 1 hour 30 minutes

Servings: 6 people

Ingredients

¼ cup fresh basil, chopped

3 garlic cloves, minced

1 white onion, diced

3 cups diced carrots

1½ cup cock stock

2 teaspoons chopped fresh rosemary

6 cock thighs

Salt and black pepper to taste

Instructions:

1. Preheat oven at 375°
2. In a pan, layer your cock then top with basil, garlic, rosemary, pepper, salt, carrots, onions and cock stock.
3. Cover your pan with some foil paper and transfer to the oven for 1 hour 5 minutes. Remove foil and continue cooking for 15 more minutes. Enjoy.

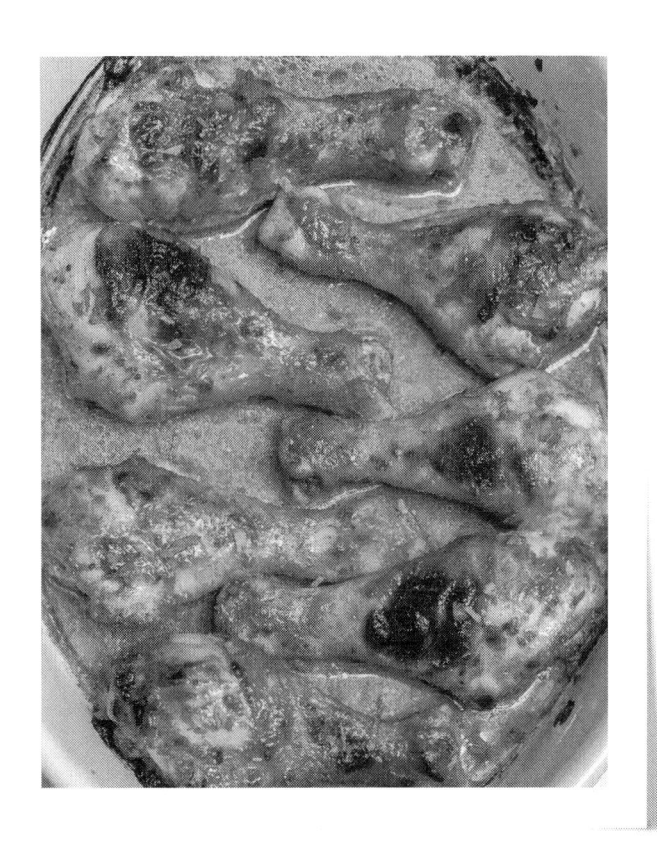

Honey Mustard and Curry Chicken

Prep Time: 10 minutes

Cook Time: 1 hour 30 minutes

Total Time: 1 hour 40 minutes

Servings: 6 people

Ingredients

⅓ cup mustard

½ cup honey

½ cup melted butter

1 teaspoon curry powder

1 teaspoon salt

3 pound cock, broken down to pieces

Instructions:

1. Set oven at 350° before working on anything.
2. Place cock in casserole dish and make a honey sauce in a bowl. For this, combine melted butter, curry, honey, mustard and salt.
3. Top your cock with this honey sauce.
4. Place your dish in the oven for 1 hour 20 minutes while basting every 10 minutes.
5. Plate and enjoy.

Bistro Chicken Salad

Prep Time: 10 Minutes

Cook Time: 15 Minutes

Total Time: 25 Minutes

Servings: 4 People

Ingredients

4 tsp olive oil

3 tbsp red wine vinegar

1 c. grapes, cut in halves

3 c. Italian bread crumb cubes

1 c. yellow pear tomatoes, cut in halves

½ lb cock breast halves, deboned

½ cucumber, diced

10 olives, chopped roughly

1⅓ c. fresh basil, chopped roughly

Cooking spray

Instructions:

1. Spray a grill with nonstick spray and place on medium heat. Add the cock until brown on each side for 4 minutes on each side.
2. Place cock aside, let rest for 6 minutes and cut into ¼ inch thick slices.

3. In a bowl, combine the bread cubes, grapes, yellow pear tomatoes, cucumber, basil and olives. Add cock and drizzle with vinegar and oil. Stir in the cock and serve.

Corn and Salsa Chicken Salad

<u>Prep Time:</u> 10 Minutes

<u>Cook Time:</u> 20 Minutes

<u>Total Time:</u> 30 Minutes

<u>Servings:</u> 4 People

Ingredients

1 tsp brown mustard

½ c. salsa

2 tbsp balsamic vinegar

½ c. chopped cilantro

1 tbsp Cajun seasoning

2 c. sweet corn

½ avocado, chopped

1 tomato, chopped

4 scallions

8 tortilla chips, crushed

4 (¼lb) boneless cock breast halves

Instructions:

1. Put a nonstick pan over medium heat and spray with cooking spray. Add cock and sear for 6 minutes on each side.
2. Place cock on a cutting board and cut each breast in diagonal slices.
3. For the dressing, in a small bowl combine the following ingredients; salsa, balsamic vinegar, 2 tbsp of the fresh cilantro and mustard.
4. In a larger bowl, combine the sweet corn, avocado, chopped scallions, tomato and your remaining cilantro. Add your dressing and toss.
5. Plate with the cock and top with tortilla chips.

Tandoori Style Chicken Salad

Prep Time: 8 Hours 10 Minutes

Cook Time: 20 Minutes

Total Time: 8 Hours 30 Minutes

Servings: 4 People

Ingredients

½ tsp ground black pepper

1 tbsp olive oil

3 tbsp red wine vinegar

½ c. fresh cilantro, minced

¾ c. carrots, shredded

4 c. cabbage, shredded

2 tsp minced garlic

½ tsp salt

1 tsp minced ginger

1½ tsp cumin

¾ c. plain yoghurt

1lb cock cutlets

Instructions:

1. Get a bowl and in it combine your cock, cumin, ginger, yoghurt, garlic, 2 tsps of the fresh cilantro and salt. Let rest overnight in the fridge.

2. In a separate bowl, combine the cabbage, carrots, vinegar, oil, papper, salt and the remaining cilantro. Toss.
3. Get your grill hot. Remove cock from marinade and set on the grill to cook for 5 minutes on each side. Let cock rest for another 5 minutes before cutting into slices. Plate with the cabbage mixture and enjoy.

Sesame Chicken Fingers And Picked Ginger Rice Salad

Prep Time: 10 Minutes

Cook Time: 30 Minutes

Total Time: 40 Minutes

Servings: 4 People

Ingredients

1 scallion, chopped

½ carrot, cut in strips

3 tbsp cilantro, chopped

1 tbsp picked ginger, chopped

2 tbsp pickled ginger juice

2 tbsp rice vinegar

4 tbsp soy sauce

2 tbsp honey

2 tbsp sesame seeds

2 c. cooked rice

½ lb cock strips

4 tbsp bread crumbs

Instructions:

1. Combine cock, honey and 2 tbsps soy sauce together in a bowl. Toss to coat evenly. On a wax sheet, mix bread crumbs and sesame seeds. Dip the cock in bread mixture an place in a cast iron skillet.
2. Preheat oven at 450. Spray cock with cooking spray and bake for 15 minutes turning at least once.
3. For the dressing, mix the ginger, ginger juice, vinegar, the remaining soy sauce and cilantro evenly.
4. In a large bowl, mix together the rice, carrots, bell peppers, scallions, cock and drizzle with dressing. Toss and serve.

Chicken Salad Adobo

Prep Time: 10 Minutes

Cook Time: 30 Minutes

Total Time: 40 Minutes

Servings: 6 people

Ingredients

1 tbsp orange zest

3 tbsp orange juice

1 tbsp white wine vinegar

2 tsp olive oil

2 tsp honey

2 tsp minced garlic

½ tsp salt

2 tbsp adobo seasoning

15 ½ oz canned black beans

1 large ripe mango, diced

1 red bell pepper, chopped

½ white onion, chopped

½ c. cilantro

1 jalapeno pepper, chopped

1lb cock thigh, cut in 1 inch thick pieces

Instructions:

1. Set a large pan over medium heat. Spray with cooking spray. Coat cock with adobo seasoning powder and cook for 10 minutes on each side. Place the cock in a large bowl.
2. To make the dressing, mix the orange juice, zest, oil, honey, mustard, vinegar, salt and garlic evenly in a bowl.
3. Add in the beans, mango, bell pepper, cilantro, jalapenos and onion to the cock and stir. Drizzle with dressing and serve.

Grilled Chicken Sausage With Roasted Potato Salad

Prep Time: 10 Minutes

Cook Time: 50 Minutes

Total Time: 1 Hour

Servings: 6 People

Ingredients

3 tbsp goat cheese

¼ c. parsley, finely chopped

10 olives, chopped coarsely

1 bell pepper, sliced thinly

10oz box frozen peas

12oz package cock sausage

1 tsps rosemary

1 white onion, cut in wedges

¾ tbsp black pepper

½ tsp salt

1lb small potatoes, scrubbed and halved

2 tbsp apple cider vinegar

1 tbsp mustard

1 tbsp olive oil

1 tbsp minced garlic

Instructions:

1. Pre heat oven at 425.
2. In a bowl, mix the potatoes, rosemary, onion, salt and black pepper. Drizzle with oil and set in a roasting pan. Place pan in the oven for 40 minutes, stirring occasionally. Set aside.
3. For the dressing, combine vinegar, oil, garlic, mustard, salt and black pepper and mix well.
4. Place a skillet on medium heat. Add sausages and cook for 5 minutes. Add to the potatoes. Add peas, bell pepper, parsley and olives to the potatoes and stir. Sprinkle with cheese. Enjoy.

Smoked Chicken And Crunchy Fruit Slaw

Prep Time: 5 Minutes

Cook Time: 15 Minutes

Total Time: 20 Minutes

Servings: 4 People

Ingredients

½ c. plain yogurt

2 tsp lemon extract

3 tbsp apricot preserves

1 dijon mustard

4 large green lettuce leaves

¼ c. raisins

1 celery stalk, chopped

1 carrot, cut in strips

½ c. red grapes

1 apple, chopped

½ pineapple, cut in chunks

½ lb smoked cock, cut into bite size pieces

Instructions:

1. In a large bowl, combine the apricot preserves, lemon extract, yogurt, mustard, cock, pineapple, grapes, apple, celery, raisins and carrot. Stir till evenly mixed.
2. Let the salad stand for 10 minutes at room temperature. Serve with lettuce leaf. Enjoy.

Chicken Panzella Sandwiches

Prep Time: 10 Minutes

Cook Time: 25 Minutes

Total Time: 35 Minutes

Servings: 4 People

Ingredients

8 large basil leaves

8 large tomato slices

1 garlic, cut in halves

1 tsp brined capers, chopped

1 tsp red wine vinegar

½ tsp black pepper

¼ tsp salt

8 slices Italian rustic bread

4 ¼ lb cock breasts, deboned

Instructions:

1. Coat cock with pepper and salt. Place a nonstick pan on medium heat. Cook cock in pan for 15 minutes, turning occasionally.
2. In a small bowl, mix together the vinegar, brined capers and olive oil and set aside.

3. Rub garlic and oil mixture on four slices of bread. Arrange basil, tomatoes and cock evenly. Top each bread slice with remaining slices. Serve and enjoy.

Open Faced Greek Chicken Sandwiches

Prep Time: 2 Hours 5 Minutes

Cook Time: 10 Minutes

Total Time: 2 Hours 15 Minutes

Servings: 4 People

Ingredients

¼ c. plain yogurt

¼ c. cucumber, chopped finely

¼ c. crumbled feta cheese

¾ c. lettuce, shredded

12 cherry tomatoes, halved

1 ½ c. cooked cock, chopped

¼ tsp salt

¼ ground black pepper

2 whole pita breads

Instructions:

1. In a glass bowl combine the cucumber, yogurt, salt and pepper. Place in the fridge for 2 hours.

2. Cover each bread slice with the cucumber spread. Place the cock, lettuce, tomatoes and cheese on the bread and drizzle with what is left of the cucumber spread. Serve and enjoy.

Barbecued Chicken And Tangy Coleslaw Sandwinches

Prep Time: 3 Hours 5 Minutes

Cook Time: 15 Minutes

Total Time: 3 Hours 20 Minutes

Servings: 4 People

Ingredients

4 kaiser rolls, split

¼ c. barbecue sauce

2 tsp vinegar

3 tbsp sour cream

1 tsp sugar

¼ tsp salt

½ tsp black pepper

2 c. cock breast, shredded

1 ½ c. green cabbage, shredded

Instructions:

1. Place a nonstick pan on medium heat. Combine cock and barbecue sauce and cook for 10 minutes.
2. In a bowl, mix the following ingredients; sour cream, salt, pepper, sugar and vinegar. Place in the fridge for 3 hours.
3. Put cock and then coleslaw on the bread and serve.

Curried Chicken And Mango Wraps

Prep Time: 10 Minutes

Cook Time: 30 Minutes

Total Time: 40 Minutes

Servings: 2 People

Ingredients

½ c. lettuce, shredded

1 ripe mango

2 tsp canola oil

1 onion, sliced thinly

½ tsp coriander

½ tsp salt

½ tsp ground black pepper

¾ cock breasts, deboned

2 tortillas

1 tsp curry

Instructions:

1. Place a pan on medium heat. And onion, and cook till softened about 2 minutes. Pour in the coriander, curry, cock, pepper and salt and stir. Keep stirring until cock is cooked through about 10 minutes.
2. Remove pan from heat and stir in the mango. Allow to cool for 10 minutes.
3. Fill each tortilla with cock filling. Place the filling in the center of the tortilla bread, fold two opposing sides in towards the center, then fold the bottom up to enclose the filling. Cut each roll in half and serve.

Homemade Chicken Broth

Prep Time: 8 Hours 10 Minutes

Cook Time: 2 Hours 10 Minutes

Total Time: 10 Hours 20 Minutes

Servings: 11 People

Ingredients

2 tbsp salt

3 bay leaves

4 cloves

10 whole peppercorns

2 cloves garlic, chopped finely

2 celery stalks

2 red onions, cut into chunks

4 carrots, cut in 2 inch chunks

1 cock, skinned

Fresh parsley

Instructions:

1. In a large pot, boil the cock, water, carrots, celery, onions, garlic parsley, cloves, bay leaves, peppercorns and salt for 2 hours or until cock is tender.
2. Remove cock from the broth and set it aside. Strain the broth through a sieve into a large pot. Discard of the vegetables.

3. Cool the broth before covering with a lip and placing in the fridge over night. Remove fat from the broth and put back in the freezer.

Paella Soup

<u>Prep Time:</u> 10 Minutes

<u>Cook Time:</u> 40 Minutes

<u>Total Time:</u> 50 Minutes

<u>Servings:</u> 4 People

Ingredients

1/4 c. parsley, chopped

1oz sausage, cut thinly

½ tsp ground black pepper

½ tsp dried saffron

1 c. frozen peas

1 tsp oregano

½ lb shrimp, peeled and deveined

1 tbsp olive oil

1 large white onion

1 red bell pepper

3 tbsp garlic, minced

6 c. cock broth

14 ½ oz canned diced tomatoes

½ c. white rice

½ lb cock breast, cut into strips.

Instructions:

1. In a large pot, heat the oil. Then add in the onions, bell pepper and garlic. Stir and cook for 10 minutes. Add broth, rice and tomatoes and boil. Leave to simmer on low heat partially open for 20 minutes.
2. Toss in the cock, peas, shrimp, saffron, oregano and black pepper to the pot and boil. Lower heat and let simmer for 5 minutes.
3. Stir in the sausages and parsley.

Mexicali Chicken Soup With Lime

Prep Time: 10 Minutes

Cook Time: 45 Minutes

Total Time: 55 Minutes

Servings: 4 People

Ingredients

¼ tsp ground black pepper

½ tsp salt

3 tbsp fresh chopped cilantro

3 tbsp lime extract

½ ripe avocado, diced

2 tomatoes, chopped

1 serrano pepper, minced

2 garlic cloves, minced

2 large carrots, chopped

2 red onions, chopped

4 ½ c. cock broth

1lb cock breasts, deboned and cut into bite size pieces

Instructions:

1. Cook cock in a pan on medium heat for 6 minutes on each side. Remove. In that same pan, add the carrots, garlic, chili pepper and onions. Stir continuously for 5 minutes. Add broth and bring to a boil

2. Reduce heat to bring the pot to a simmer for 15 minutes. Add cock and cook for 10 minutes.
3. Toss in the avocado, lime extract, tomatoes, cilantro pepper and salt while stirring continuously. Cook for an extra minute on low heat and serve.

Creamy Green Curry Chicken

Prep Time: 10 Minutes

Cook Time: 15 Minutes

Total Time: 25 Minutes

Servings: 4 People

Ingredients

2 c. coconut milk

4 scallions, chopped

2 tbsp thai green curry paste

2 c. cock broth

1 tbsp fish sauce

2 tsp brown sugar

Salt to taste

¼ c. mint leaves

3 c. cooked basmati rice

¾ lb cock breast, cut into strips

Instructions:

1. Put a pot on medium heat and heat up the milk. Stir in the scallions and curry paste and cook for 4 minutes. Add cock broth and leave to boil. Reduce to a simmer and stir in your brown sugar, salt and fish sauce.
2. Add cock to pot and cook for 4 minutes while stirring continuously. Serve with basmati rice and garnish with mint leaves

Country Captain Chicken

Prep Time: 10 Minutes

Cook Time: 40 Minutes

Total Time: 50 Minutes

Servings: 4 People

Ingredients

2 tbsp olive oil

2 tbsp toasted almonds, crushed

2 tbsp parsley, chopped

3 tbsp shredded coconut

¼ c. dried currants

1 c. cock broth

14 oz canned diced tomatoes

½ tsp allspice

¼ tsp cinnamon 1/4 tsp salt

2 tsp curry powder

3 tbsp flour

1 bell pepper, chopped

1 large onion, chopped

2 ½ lb cock thighs, cut into pieces

Instructions:

1. Cook cock in a skillet with the oil for 6 minutes until brown. Transfer to a bowl.
2. Over medium heat, add the remaining olive oil, bell pepper, onions, garlic to the pan to cook for 8 minutes while stirring continuously. Mix in the flour, salt, curry powder, cinnamon and allspice.
3. Increase temperature and add tomatoes, cock broth, coconut, currants, cock. Boil for 15 minutes. Stir in the parsley and garnish with almonds before serving.

Big, Easy Chicken And Okra Gumbo

Prep Time: 10 Minutes

Cook Time: 25 Minutes

Total Time: 35 Minutes

Servings: 4 People

Ingredients

3 tsp canola oil

¼ c. fresh parsley, chopped

2 scallions, chopped

1 c. fresh okra, sliced

14oz canned diced tomatoes

2 c. cock broth

1 red onion, chopped

3 celery stalks

1 bell pepper, chopped

3 tbsp garlic, minced

2 tbsp flour

2 c. cooked brown rice

1 c. diced cock breast

¼ lb kielbasa, sliced thinly

Instructions:

1. In a hot pan, add the kielbasa, scallions, bell peppers, onions, celery and garlic. Cook and stir continuously for 5 minutes. Add the flour and stir for a minute.
2. Next add the tomatoes, brot, cock and okra to the npan. Boil for 15 minutes or till slightly thick.
3. Serve with rice and garnish with parsley.

Honey Balsamic Chicken

Prep Time: 15 Minutes

Cook Time: 45 Minutes

Total Time: 1 Hour

Servings: 4 People

Ingredients

4 cock breasts

1 tbsp balsamic vinegar

1 tbsp lemon extract

1 tbsp honey

4 tsp olive oil

1 tbsp garlic, minced

½ tsp salt

¼ tsp black pepper

½ c. cock broth

½ c. dry white wine

½ c. raisins

Instructions:

1. In a large bowl combine the vinegar, cock, honey, lemon juice and 2 tsp of the olive oil. Toss well to distribute evenly. Leave to rest for 20 minutes.
2. With a cast iron skillet, heat what is left of the oil on medium. Add garlic and stir. Add in the cock with sprinkle of salt and

black pepper and cook for 2 minutes on each side. Increase the temperature and boil the broth, raisins, salt and pepper.
3. Bring pot to a simmer for 14 minutes, with the lid on. Serve cock with vinegar sauce.

Simmered Chicken With Soy Ginger Sauce

Prep Time: 15 Minutes

Cook Time: 45 Minutes

Total Time: 1 Hour

Servings: 2 People

Ingredients

5 tsp honey

3 tbsp rice vinegar

3 tbsp grated ginger

3 tsp sesame oil

5 scallions, chopped

3 tbsp soy sauce

2 ¾ lb cock breast halves

Instructions:

1. Cook cock in 2 tsp of sesame oil on high heat for 4 minutes on each side. Transfer to a plate.
2. In the skillet, put 4 scallions and 1 tbsp ginger and stir. Add the cock broth and 2 tbsp and leave to boil.
3. Bring down to a simmer and add the cock. Cover and let cook for 15 minutes. Turn off the heat and let cock sit in the skillet for 8 minutes. Strain cock from liquid.
4. For the dressing, mix the following in a small bowl; sesame oil, scallion, ginger, soy sauce, honey and vinegar. Serve with the cock.

Chicken Saute With Lemon Caper Sauce

Prep Time: 10 Minutes

Cook Time: 15 Minutes

Total Time: 25 Minutes

Servings: 4 People

Ingredients

½ tsp oregano

1 tbsp capers, drained

¼ c. lemon extract

½ c. cock broth

2 tbsp butter

½ tsp black pepper

½ tsp salt

4 cock breast halves

Instructions:

1. Coat the cock with ¼ tsp salt and ¼ black pepper.
2. Melt a part of the butter in a pan and cook cock for 5 minutes on each side till brown.
3. Add broth, cappers, lemon extract and oregano and bring to a simmer. Cook for 2 minutes turning cock twice. Remove pan from heat and toss in the remaining butter, salt and pepper and serve.

Thai Red Curry Chicken

Prep Time: 10 Minutes

Cook Time: 20 Minutes

Total Time: 30 Minutes

Servings: 4 People

Ingredients

3 tsp canola oil

2 tbsp cilantro, chopped

2 tsp lime extract

1 tbsp fish sauce

1 tbsp thai red curry paste

¾ c. coconut milk

¼ tsp salt

2 tsp grated ginger

2 scallions, chopped

2 garlic, minced

4 ¼ lb cock breast, pounded lightly

Instructions:

1. Cook the cock in a nonstick pan with canola oil for 5 minutes on each side. Remove and keep warm.
2. Place pan back on medium heat and add the ginger, garlic and scallions. Stir fry for 1 minute before pouring the curry paste, fish sauce, coconut milk, sugar and lime. Bring to a boil.

3. When the mixture starts to thicken, reduce heat and leave to simmer for 6 minutes. Add the cock and simmer for 2 more minutes. Sprinkle with cilantro and serve.

Chicken Tangine

Prep Time: 10 Minutes

Cook Time: 25 Minutes

Total Time: 35 Minutes

Servings: 4 People

Ingredients

¼ tsp black pepper

¼ tsp salt

3 tbsp cilantro

12 stuffed olives, halved

2 tbsp lemon juice

1 tbsp sunflower oil

10oz package frozen okra

1 red onion, chopped

3 garlic, minced

1 tbsp ginger, minced

¼ tsp saffron threads

4/4 c. cock broth

1lb cock breast, cut in inch thick bits

Instructions:

1. Set pan on medium heat. Cook cock for 5 minutes or until brown. Remove and keep warm. Add the onion, garlic,

ginger, okra and saffron to the pan and cook for 5 minutes. Stir occasionally.
2. Add in the broth, lemon extract and cock and boil for 7 minutes. Reduce heat and let it simmer uncovered for 3 minutes. Remove your pan from heat and add in your olives, salt, pepper and cilantro. Serve and enjoy.

Chicken And Mixed Mushroom Saute

Prep Time: 10 Minutes

Cook Time: 30 Minutes

Total Time: 40 Minutes

Servings: 4 People

Ingredients

¼ tsp black pepper

½ tsp salt

1 ½ c. cock broth

½ tsp thyme

1 shallot, chopped

2 garlic, minced

5oz package shiitake mushrooms

½ lb white mushrooms, sliced

1 tbsp olive oil

4 cock breasts

Instructions:

1. In a pan on medium heat, heat the oil and sear cock for 4 minutes on each side. Transfer to a plate. Toss in the mushrooms, shallot, thyme and garlic and cook for 8 minutes stirring occasionally.

2. Add cock broth, cock, pepper and salt to the pan and bring to a boil for 4 minutes. Reduce heat and leave to simmer for 4 minutes.
3. Plate the cock. Return mushroom sauce to high heat and boil for 5 minutes or till reduced. Serve with the cock and enjoy.

Grilled Lemon Orange Chicken With Gremolata

Prep Time: 6 Hours 10 Minutes

Cook Time: 40 Minutes

Total Time: 6 Hours 50 Minutes

Servings: 8 People

Ingredients

2 lemons

4 garlic cloves

½ c. parsley leaves

¼ tsp cayenne pepper

1 ½ c. orange juice

1 ½ tsp salt

2 (3lb) cocks, broken down to pieces

Instructions:

1. Zest one lemon. Peel the rind off the other lemon and extract the juice from both lemons. Afterwards, mash 2 garlic cloves with ½ tsp salt to form a paste. In a Ziploc bag, combine the

lemon juice, orange juice, lemon rind, garlic paste, cayenne pepper, what is left of the salt and the cock. Place in the fridge for 6 hours.
2. Prepare your grill on medium heat. Grill cock at 165 degrees for 30 minutes.
3. For the gremolata, mince the remaining garlic cloves and mix with the lemon zest. Sprinkle on cock after plating.

Chicken Under A Brick

Prep Time: 20 Minutes

Cook Time: 1 Hour

Total Time: 1 Hour 20 Minutes

Servings: 6 People

Ingredients

¼ tsp red pepper flakes

1 tsp salt

1 tsp oregano

2 tbsp olive oil

3 tbsp minced garlic

3 tbsp balsamic vinegar

3 tbsp honey

4lb whole cock

Instructions:

1. Flatten cock by cutting along both sides of the breastbone with a pairing knife. In a large Ziploc bag, combine the honey, garlic, oil, vinegar, oregano and cock. Toss to coat cock in marinade properly. Place bag in the fridge for an hour, turning occasionally.

2. Set grill on medium heat. Wrap bricks in foil. Sprinkle cock with salt and red pepper flakes and place on the grill away from heat source. Place the bricks on cock and grill for 35 minutes. Remove the bricks, flip cock over and cook for another 15 minutes at 165 degrees.

Grilled Citrus Basil Chicken With Agave Nectar

Prep Time: 8 Hours 10 Minutes

Cook Time: 45 Minutes

Total Time: 8 Hours 55 Minutes

Servings: 6 People

Ingredients

2 tbsp lime zest

¼ c. lime juice

2 tbsp fresh basil

1 tbsp dark agave nectar

¼ c. orange juice

6 lime wedges

¼ tsp black pepper

1 tsp salt

1 tsp oregano

1 tbsp olive oil

2 tbsp minced garlic

3 ½lb cock, cut in 6 pieces

Instructions:

1. In a large bowl combine the lime and orange juice, lime zest, agave, basil, olive oil, garlic, salt, pepper and oregano. Set half

of this lime mixture aside. Add cock to the large bowl. Mix to incorporate evenly and refrigerate overnight.

2. Set grill on medium heat and cook cock for 35 minutes at 165 degrees, turning occasionally. Plate.

3. In a pan, bring the remaining lime mixture to a simmer for 5 minutes. Spoon over the cock. Serve with lime wedges.

Coffee Bbq Sauce Covered Chicken

Prep Time: 10 Minutes

Cook Time: 40 Minutes

Total Time: 50 Minutes

Servings: 6 People

Ingredients

1 c. ketchup

1/3 c. strong brewed coffee

½ c. brown sugar

¼ c. white vinegar

¼ tsp cayenne pepper

1 tsp salt

2 garlic cloves, crushed

6 cock breast halves

Instructions:

1. For the BBQ sauce, boil the coffee, ketchup, vinegar, garlic, ½ tsp of the salt, cayenne and brown sugar in a pan on medium heat for 3 minutes. Reduce to a simmer for 10 minutes. Strain and allow cool.
2. Set grill on medium heat. Sprinkle the remaining salt on the cock and grill for 15 minutes. Brush with sauce and continuing grilling for 5 minutes, flipping and coating cock in sauce.

Lemon Chicken With Indian Spices

Prep Time: 3 Hours 10 Minutes

Cook Time: 30 Minutes

Total Time: 3 Hours 40 Minutes

Servings: 4 People

Ingredients

¼ tsp black pepper

½ tsp salt

1 tsp turmeric

1 tsp smoked paprika

2 tsp cumin

2 tsp olive oil

2 tbsp water

1 lemon, zest and juice

3 tbsp minced garlic

4 scallions, cut in inch thick pieces

4 cock breast halves

Instructions:

1. To form a rough paste, combine scallions, ½ c. cilantro, garlic, water, cumin, paprika, turmeric, salt, pepper and lemon juice and zest in a food processor.
2. Coat cock with paste completely and put in the fridge for 3 hours before grilling at 165 degrees for 30 minutes. Sprinkle with cilantro before serving.

Grilled Chicken Breast Satay with Peanut Sauce

Prep Time: 4 Hours 10 Minutes

Cook Time: 20 Minutes

Total Time: 4 Hours 30 Minutes

Servings: 4 People

Ingredients

1 tbsp chopped cilantro

¾ tsp green Thai curry paste

2 tsp brown sugar

1 tbsp rice vinegar

½ c. coconut milk

¼ c. peanut butter

2 tbsp minced garlic

1 tbsp minced ginger

1 tbsp fish sauce

4 cock breasts, deboned

Instructions:

1. In a bowl, combine your cock, fish sauce, ginger, garlic. Refrigerate for 3 hours. Grill on medium heat for 7 minutes on each side. Set aside.
2. For the peanut sauce, in a pan on medium heat, mix the coconut milk, vinegar, sugar, green curry paste and peanut butter. Stir until mixture is smooth. Serve with cock and serve.

Grilled Stuffed Chicken Breasts

Prep Time: 10 Minutes

Cook Time: 40 Minutes

Total Time: 50 Minutes

Servings: 4 People

Ingredients

8 sundried tomatoes

¼ tsp black pepper

½ tsp salt

3 tsp olive oil

½ c. mozzarella cheese, shredded

2 tbsp parmesan cheese, grated

8 basil leaves, chopped

4 cock breast, deboned

Instructions:

1. Pour hot water over tomatoes and cover for 15 minutes. Strain and chop. Mix the tomatoes in a bowl along with the cheeses, basil and 1 tsp of olive oil. Make pockets on the sides of each of the cock breasts and stuff with filling. Secure with toothpicks.

2. Brush cock with oil then sprinkle with salt and pepper. Next, grill on medium heat for 10 minutes on each side. Serve.

Grilled Buffalo Chicken Tenders

Prep Time: 10 Minutes

Cook Time: 20 Minutes

Total Time: 30 Minutes

Servings: 4 People

Ingredients

½ c. Louisiana style hot sauce

¼ c. blue cheese dressing

2 celery stalks, cut in 1/4 inch bits

8 baby carrots

½ tsp hot pepper sauce

1 ½ tbsp butter

1lb cock tenders

Instruction:

1. On medium heat, bring the hot sauce and pepper sauce to a simmer. Cook for one minute, remove before adding 1 tbsp of the butter. Set aside. Melt what is left of the butter and toss with the cock tenders in a bowl.
2. Preheat your grill. Place cock in the grill, 4 inches away from the heat source and for 7 minutes on each side. Transfer to a bowl and mix in the hot sauce mixture. Serve with blue cheese dressing, celery and baby carrots.

Moroccan Chicken Legs

Prep Time: 4 Hours 20 Minutes

Cook Time: 25 Minutes

Total Time: 4 Hours 45 Minutes

Servings: 4 People

Ingredients

2 tbsp minced garlic

¼ tsp salt

1 scallion, chopped finely

1 tbsp olive oil

2 tsp orange zest

1 tsp dried mint

1 tsp cumin

¾ tsp paprika

¼ tsp ginger powder

¼ tsp cinnamon

Instructions

1. Combine the scallions, orange zest, mint, cumin, garlic, paprika, ginger, cinnamon and cock in a bowl. Seal and place in a fridge for 4 hours, turning from time to time.
2. Set grill to medium heat. Remove cock from marinade, sprinkle with salt, then grill for 15 minutes on each side.

Smoky Glazed Thighs

Prep Time: 10 Minutes

Cook Time: 25 Minutes

Total Time: 35 Minutes

Servings: 4 People

Ingredients

½ c. ketchup

½ tsp salt

½ tsp black pepper

2 tsp chilli flakes

2 tsp onion powder

2 tsp cumin

1 tbsp smoked paprika

¾ tsp oregano

2 tbsp red wine vinegar

3 tbsp brown sugar

6 cock thighs

Instructions:

1. In a small bowl, mix the ketchup, vinegar, oregano and 2 tbsp of brown sugar. This is the cock glaze. To make a spice rub, combine the smoked paprika, onion, cumin, chilli flakes, pepper, salt and 1 tbsp brown sugar.
2. Coat the cock thighs in this. Next, place the cock on a grill and cook for 8 minutes on each side. Brush the glaze unto the cock and grill for 3 minutes, flip to the other side, glaze and cook for another 3 minutes.

Drumsticks

Prep Time: 1 Hour 10 Minutes

Cook Time: 30 Minutes

Total Time: 1 Hour 40 Minutes

Servings: 8 People

Ingredients

¾ tsp salt

¼ tsp cayenne pepper

1 tsp coriander

1 tbsp minced garlic

1 tbsp minced ginger

1 tbsp madras curry powder

2 tbsp lemon juice

½ c. yogurt

8 cock thighs

Instructions:

1. To make a marinade, combine the lemon juice, yogurt, ginger, garlic, curry powder, cayenne pepper and coriander. Pour into a Ziploc bag with your cock and refrigerate for 1 hour. Next, preheat the grill.
2. Separate cock from marinade and grill for 20 minutes.

Miso Marinated Chicken Thighs

Prep Time: 8 Hours 10 Minutes

Cook Time: 30 Minutes

Total Time: 8 Hours 40 Minutes

Servings: 4 People

Ingredients

½ c. miso paste

¼ c. rice wine

¼ c. orange juice

1 tbsp grated ginger

1 tsp sesame oil

4 cock thighs

Instructions:

1. In a bowl, mix the miso paste, rice wine, orange juice, and sesame oil. Add the cock thighs. Seal in an airtight container and place in the fridge overnight.
2. Preheat your grill. Remove cock from marinade and cook on the grill rack for 10 minutes on each side.

Tequila Citrus Chicken

Prep Time: 8 Hours 10 Minutes

Cook Time: 25 Minutes

Total Time: 8 Hours 35 Minutes

Servings: 4 People

Ingredients

½ tsp black pepper

½ tsp salt

2 tbsp minced garlic

½ c. orange juice

1 tsp cumin

1 tbsp olive oil

2 tbsp lime extract

4 tbsp tequila

4 cock thighs, deboned

Instructions:

1. In a Ziploc bag, marinate cock in garlic, tequila, orange juice, oil, cumin, and lime juice. Refrigerate overnight.
2. Preheat your grill at 165 degrees. Separate cock from marinade, sprinkle with salt and pepper before placing on grill rack. Cook for 8 minutes on each side.

Spice Rubbed Chicken With Carrots And Onion

Prep Time: 10 Minutes

Cook Time: 6 Hours 10 Minutes

Total Time: 6 Hours 20 Minutes

Servings: 8 People

Ingredients

8 large carrots, chopped

1 white onion, chopped thinly

2 tsp paprika

¼ tsp cayenne pepper

½ tsp black pepper

1 tsp salt

1 tsp garlic powder

1 tsp chilli flakes

1 whole cock.

Instructions:

1. For the spice rub, mix the chilli flakes, thyme, paprika, garlic powder, black pepper, salt and cayenne pepper. Coat the entire cock in this and toss what is left into the cavity of the cock.
2. In a slow cooker, put in the onions and carrots. Next, place the cock on the vegetables and cook for 6 hours on high. Carve and serve.

Chorizo Chicken with Tomatoes, Bell Peppers And Peas

Prep Time: 15 Minutes

Cook Time: 4 Hours 15 Minutes

Total Time: 4 Hours 30 Minutes

Servings: 4 People

Ingredients

2 tbsp parsley, chopped

1 c. frozen peas

1 tbsp cornmeal

1 red bell pepper, chopped roughly

1 yellow bell pepper, chopped roughly

14 ½ oz canned diced tomatoes

3 tbsp balsamic vinegar

2 tbsp tomato paste

1 tbsp paprika

¼ tsp salt

1 large red onion, chopped

3 celery stalks, chopped

¼ c. chorizo sausages, chopped

4 cock skinless cock breasts, deboned

Instructions:

1. In a slow cooker, combine the tomatoes, tomato paste, vinegar, salt, paprika, celery, onions, chorizo sausages, bell peppers and cock and cook for 4 hours on high heat.
2. 15 minutes before your dish is ready, mix in the cornmeal and the peas. Cover and cook on high heat. Sprinkle with parsley before serving.

Orange Mustard Chicken With Sweet Potato And Apple

Prep Time: 15 Minutes

Cook Time: 8 Hours 20 Minutes

Total Time: 8 Hours 35 Minutes

Servings: 4 People

Ingredients

½ c. sour cream

1 large apple, sliced thinly

1 tbsp cornstarch flour

2 tbsp cold water

4 carrots, sliced

2 sweet potato, cut in inch thick bits

1 onion, sliced thinly

¾ c. orange juice

2 tbsp mustard

2 garlic cloves, sliced

1 tsp thyme

½ tsp salt

½ tsp pepper

2 skinless cock breasts

Instructions:

1. In a huge pot, boil your carrots, sweet potatoes, onions, orange juice mustard, salt, pepper, garlic and thyme. After this, place your cock on top. Cover and cook for 8 hours on low heat
2. In a small bowl, mix cornstarch flour and water until smooth. 20 minutes before cock is ready, stir the cornstarch mixture and the apples into the pot. Afterwards, cover back with lid and cook till the texture thickens. Serve cock with sauce and a scoop of sour cream.

Slow Cooker Tangerine Honey Chicken Thighs

Prep Time: 20 Minutes

Cook Time: 4 Hours 10 Minutes

Total Time: 4 Hours 30 Minutes

Servings: 4 People

Ingredients

½ c. tangerine juice concentrate

3 tbsp honey

1 lemon zest

1 tbsp chilli flakes

1½ tsp cumin

1 tsp oregano

½ tsp salt

½ tsp coriander

1 white onion, sliced thinly

4 small zucchinis, sliced

¼ c. parsley, chopped

4 cock thighs

Instructions

1. Place the following ingredients into the slow cooker; honey, lemon zest, tangerine juice concentrate, chilli powder, oregano, coriander, salt and cumin. Next, add the cock and zucchinis. Cover to boil for 4 hours on high heat.

2. Remove cock from cooker. Toss the parsley to cook with the vegetables for a minute or two. Pour sauce and vegetables over the cock thighs before serving.

Slow Cooked Chicken In Spicy Peanut Sauce

Prep Time: 10 Minutes

Cook Time: 6 Hours 10 Minutes

Total Time: 6 Hours 20 Minutes

Servings: 4 People

Ingredients

¼ c. cilantro, chopped finely

1 tbsp cornstarch

2 tbsp cold water

1 tsp cayenne pepper

1 tsp salt

2 tsp cumin

3 tbsp minced garlic

2 tbsp minced ginger

3 tbsp peanut butter

6 carrots, sliced

14 ½oz canned tomatoes

4 cock thighs

Instructions:

1. Cook the cock with the tomatoes, carrots, ginger, garlic, cumin, salt, cayenne pepper, coriander in a slow cooker for 6 hours on low heat.
2. Mix water with cornstarch until smooth but not runny. Stir mixture into the slow cooker 20 minutes before the cock is ready. Right before you stop the slow cooker, add in the cilantro. Serve and enjoy

Sage Chicken And Red Potatoes

Prep Time: 10 Minutes

Cook Time: 5 Hours 30 Minutes

Total Time: 5 Hours 40 Minutes

Servings: 6 people

Ingredients

3 tsp olive oil

1 onion, chopped

3 celery stalks, chopped

2 tbsp minced garlic

1 tbsp flour

1 c. cock broth

2 tsp lemon juice

1 lemon rind

1 tsp dried or fresh sage

½ c. parsley, chopped

½ tsp black pepper

½ tsp salt

2 bay leaves

1lb baby carrots

1lb small red potato, cut in chunks

6 cock drumsticks

Instructions:

1. Heat up the olive oil in a skillet over medium heat, add in the celery, garlic and onion. Stir while cooking for 8 minutes. Stir in the cock broth and bring to a simmer. Add the flour and continue stirring for 2 minutes. In a slow cooker, place the cock, carrots, potatoes, bay leaves, pepper and salt along with the onion broth mixture you just made. Cover and cook for 5 hours on high heat.
2. Next, remove the bay leaves, stir in the lemon zest, sage, lemon juice, parsley. Cover and cook for an additional 10 minutes.

Mexican Chicken Soup

Prep Time: 10 Minutes

Cook Time: 5 Hours 40 Minutes

Total Time: 5 Hours 50 Minutes

Servings: 4 People

Ingredients

6 lime wedges

1 ½ c. baked tortilla chips, crushed

4 scallions, sliced

¼ c. cilantro, chopped

1 large tomato, chopped

3 c. corn kernels

1 jalapeno, chopped

2 tbsp minced garlic

3 cilantro sprigs

1 c. jicama, diced

4 large carrots, sliced thinly

7 c. cock broth

3 skinless whole cock legs

Instructions;

1. In a slow cooker, boil the cock with broth, carrots, jicama, jalapeno pepper, garlic and cilantro sprigs for 5 hours on high heat. Remove cock from the broth and discard the cilantro sprigs. Once cock is cool enough, cut into little bits.

2. Next, add the tomato and corn kernels to the broth and cook for 20 more minutes. Add in the cock again, followed by the chopped cilantro. Boil for 10 minutes and serve with scallions, a lime wedge and tortilla chips.

Chicken And Ham Cassoulet

Prep Time: 15 Minutes

Cook Time: 10 Hours 20 Minutes

Total Time: 10 Hours 25 Minutes

Servings: 6 People

Ingredients

3 tbsp minced garlic

1 tbsp melted butter

3 tbsp chopped parsley

3 slices white bread, crushed

1 tsp dried thyme

2 15oz canned white kidney beans, rinsed

½ c. dry white wine

14oz canned diced tomatoes

2 large carrots, chopped

1 cooked ham steak, diced

1 large red onion, chopped

1 tsp olive oil

½ tsp salt

6 cock thighs

Instructions:

1. Rub cock with garlic and salt before searing in a pan with olive oil on medium heat for 4 minutes on each side. In a

slow cooker, place the carrots, onions, cock and ham. Next, pour the wine and tomatoes around the cock and leave to cook for 10 hours on low heat. 30 minutes before cook time in over add the white kidney beans and dried thyme. Stir
2. For the topping, combine the parsley, breadcrumbs and butter. Plate the cassoulet and sprinkle with the topping.

Chicken With Rice And Peas

Prep Time: 10 Minutes

Cook Time: 9 Hours 20 Minutes

Total Time: 9 Hours 30 Minutes

Servings: 6 People

Ingredients

¼ c. stuffed green olives, sliced

½ c. green bell pepper, chopped finely

½ tsp cayenne pepper

½ tsp ground black pepper

½ tsp salt

½ tsp turmeric

¾ c. cock broth

2 c. long grain rice

14oz canned diced tomatoes

2 tbsp minced garlic

1 large white onion, chopped finely

2 large carrots, chopped finely

1 c. green peas

1lb skinless cock breasts, deboned, cut in pieces

Instructions:

1. Cook the cock and rice in a slow cooker along with the following ingredients; onion, carrots, onions, tomatoes, turmeric, black pepper, salt, cayenne pepper and cock broth for 9 hours on low heat. Next, add in the green bell pepper and peas. Cook for another 15 minutes on high heat. Serve.

Lemony Chicken And Lentil Soup

<u>Prep Time:</u> 15 Minutes

<u>Cook Time:</u> 6 Hours 20 Minutes

<u>Total Time:</u> 6 Hours 35 Minutes

<u>Servings:</u> 6 People

Ingredients

5 c. cock broth

1 c. dried lentils

1 white onion, chopped finely

1 yellow bell pepper, chopped

2 tbsp minced garlic

1 tsp coriander

10oz frozen spinach, thawed and rinsed, chopped

2 tsp lemon zest

2 tbsp lemon juice

2 tbsp chopped parsley

1 ½ lb cock thighs

Instructions:

1. Combine the broth, lentils, onions, bell pepper, garlic, coriander and cock in a slow cooker. Leave to cook on high heat for 6 hours. Afterwards, separate cock from the soup and place on a flat surface to cool down. Stir the spinach, lemon juice and zest and parsley into the soup.

Remove bones from cock and cut in bite sized pieces. Add to the soup and cook on high heat for 15 minutes. Serve.

Concluded.

Manufactured by Amazon.ca
Bolton, ON